BEING "JOB-READY" IDENTIFY YOUR SKILLS, STRENGTHS, AND CAREER GOALS

by
Ronald C. Mendlin
and
Marc Polonsky
with **J. Michael Farr**

Being "Job-Ready"
Identify Your Skills, Strengths, and Career Goals

© 2000 by

Chapter 1: Ronald C. Mendlin and Marc Polonsky
Chapter 2: Ronald C. Mendlin and Marc Polonsky
Chapter 3: J. Michael Farr
Chapter 4: Ronald C. Mendlin and Marc Polonsky

Published by JIST Works, Inc.
8902 Otis Avenue
Indianapolis, IN 46216-1033

Phone: 1-800-648-JIST Fax: 1-800-JIST-FAX
E-mail: editorial@jist.com Web site: www.jist.com

Other books in JIST's *Putting the Bars Behind You* series:

The "Double You": The Person You Are and the Person You Want to Be

Job Search Tools: Resumes, Applications, and Cover Letters

Networking and Interviewing for Jobs

Keeping Your Job

An instructor's guide for the series is available separately from JIST.

The *Putting the Bars Behind You* series is derived from the *Job Search Basics* series by J. Michael Farr and Susan Christophersen.

Acquisitions Editor: Michael Cunningham
Development Editor: Lori Cates
Proofreader: Rebecca York
Interior and Cover Designer: Aleata Howard
Layout Technician: Carolyn J. Newland

Printed in the United States of America.

03 02 01 00   9 8 7 6 5 4 3 2 1

We have been careful to provide accurate information throughout this book, but it is possible that errors and omissions have been introduced. Please consider this in making any important decisions. Trust your own judgment above all else and in all things.

Trademarks: All brand names and product names used in this book are trade names, service marks, trademarks, or registered trademarks of their respective owners.

ISBN: 1-56370-705-5

About This Book

This workbook will help you find a job and adjust to life after prison. First, you will read about ideas that are important to your transition to a new life. Then you will interact with these ideas through questions and worksheets. Be sure to keep a pen or pencil handy. When you get out into the world and start looking for a job, remember what you learned here and look back through your answers as needed.

This book is one of five in JIST's *Putting the Bars Behind You* series. The following special features appear in all the books in this series:

Example. An "Example" usually features words of wisdom from real people who have been in your shoes. Read about the ways in which they are successfully making the transition from prison to the outside world.

Think About It. It's time to stop reading when you see the light bulb. Take a few minutes to think about what you just read. Answer the questions in the best way you can. Don't rush! When you are done writing, continue reading the book.

Worksheets. Worksheets are identified by the image at left. All worksheets contain clear directions to help you practice and interact with the concepts in the book.

Hints and Tips. These thoughts appear in the graphic you see at left. For extra guidance and inspiration, don't miss these boxes.

Checkpoint. When you see the clipboard, get ready to review the chapter. Answer the questions about the chapter's material. Look back and reread the pages as needed.

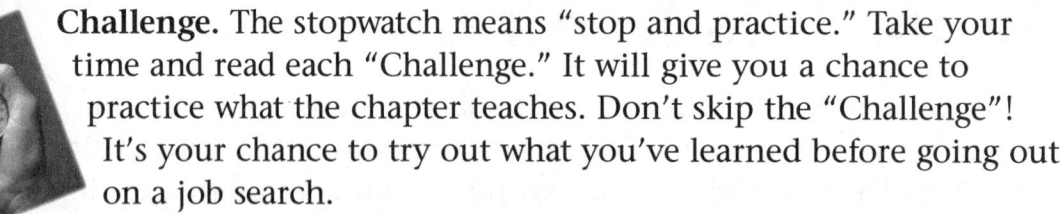

Challenge. The stopwatch means "stop and practice." Take your time and read each "Challenge." It will give you a chance to practice what the chapter teaches. Don't skip the "Challenge"! It's your chance to try out what you've learned before going out on a job search.

Good luck in your new life!

Other books in JIST's *Putting the Bars Behind You* series:

The "Double You": The Person You Are and the Person You Want to Be

Job Search Tools: Resumes, Applications, and Cover Letters

Networking and Interviewing for Jobs

Keeping Your Job

About the Authors

Ronald Clark Mendlin has over 38 years of experience in 14 business fields. He has received numerous commendations from government officials for project leadership and superior job performance. As a job developer for Northern California Service League, he has placed hundreds of state prison parolees in jobs, and has found jobs for work-furlough residents who had from six hours to three days to get a job or be sent back to prison. Mr. Mendlin, who has created his own jobs, has lectured extensively about job search methods for community organizations.

Marc Polonsky is a freelance writer who has taught college English for over 12 years. He holds master's degrees in Instructional Technologies and English, and is the author of *The Poetry Reader's Toolkit*. Mr. Polonsky has also co-taught seminars on ethics, critical thinking, public speaking, and interpersonal communication skills.

J. Michael Farr has been teaching, writing, and developing his job search techniques for over 20 years. He has written over 20 books that have sold over 2 million copies. Mr. Farr emphasizes practical, results-oriented methods that have been proven to reduce the time it takes to find a job. His writing style is friendly and clear, and his commonsense advice has made his books the most widely used in job search programs.

Contents

Acknowledgments

The authors would like to acknowledge the following individuals for their invaluable help with this project:

Lorraine Mendlin

Eve Decker

Shirley Melnicoe

Northern California Service League

Will Turner

Dennis Bellman

Barbara Grassi

Larry Braynen

Charles R. Temple

Frank Malifrando

Darro Jefferson

Melody Fountilia

Linda Koski

Patrick Ryan

Nema Williams

Kathleen Dwyer

Michael Markham

Carolyn Oliver

INTRODUCTION

Finding Out What You Have to Offer

Make no mistake: You bring many skills and strengths to the workforce. You have picked up a lot of valuable knowledge, experiences, and abilities in your life, no matter where you've been, and no matter what you think.

The purpose of this book is to help you take stock of what you have to offer. The first step toward finding a job is taking a *complete* look at the skills you have. After you have done this, you can begin to set realistic goals about what kind of work you want, what kind of career you want, and what other kinds of skills you might need to develop along the way.

It's fine to have big dreams, as long as you have a solid foundation. This book is about planting your feet, so that you can reach as high or as far as you want to.

What Work Can Do for You

Work has a great deal to offer you. It's how you "plug in" to the world. People you work with can become your good friends, because you will have interests and experiences in common with them—and because you will spend so much time together. And, of course, work pays you money. Work in the outside world pays a real wage, which you can use to buy food, clothing, and shelter, as well as other things you might want for yourself. Of course, not all jobs are equal. Some jobs pay more than others; some jobs are more pleasant than others; and, most importantly, some jobs are more appropriate for *you* than others.

Being "Job-Ready"

What does it mean to be "job-ready"? You are job-ready when you've got somewhere to stay, you've got clean clothes to wear, you've got a positive attitude, and you're clean and sober. Having your life goals and values in place is the next step. You worked on discovering your goals in book 1, *The Double You*. In this book you will learn what skills you have to offer employers.

Chapter One

Your Foundation

THE GOALS OF THIS CHAPTER ARE

❑ To look at your work and life experience and point out the skills you've gained.

❑ To learn the difference between a strength and a skill.

❑ To identify your strengths.

❑ To identify what work environment you prefer and would fit into best.

Make the Most of Your Experience

The word *experience* means, simply, anything that you have lived through. Clearly, you have lived through many things. You've had lots of experiences. Most experiences give us something that we can use later—

some skill or some knowledge. Even from unpleasant or illegal experiences, you can learn something positive. For example, somebody who has been a drug dealer knows about salesmanship and about business. Somebody who has been locked up knows something about patience and how to keep busy. These skills might come in handy when you get a job.

Even the most ordinary experiences give us skills. Taking the bus or the subway teaches you to pay attention and to organize your time in a particular way. Reading the newspaper requires that you translate printed words into images and ideas in your mind, which is a very important skill that comes in handy in many of the more pleasant jobs.

Then there are work experiences, which give you all kinds of skills. A waiter in a restaurant has to be quick with his hands, talk pleasantly to strangers, use his memory, and tolerate stress when the restaurant gets very busy or customers are rude. A store clerk has to be able to count money quickly, use a cash register, understand the organization of the store, and much more.

Think About It

List some experiences you've had. Think about the skills you gained from these experiences, or the skills you needed to do these things. Then think about other ways you could use (or have used) these same skills again.

The first two lines of the table list some other examples you can use to help you think about it.

Experiences	Skills Needed or Learned	Other Ways to Use These Skills
Loud argument with my girlfriend or boyfriend.	Had to calm myself.	I can calm myself down in any conflict situation, so that I don't do anything destructive.
Took my nephew to a baseball game.	How to talk to a six-year-old; be able to explain the game; pay attention to kid and make sure he was comfortable; buy him food when he was hungry; just give him what he needed.	I can use my ability to explain things if I want to be a teacher or trainer; I can use my skill of paying attention to kids' needs in any situation where there are other people; I can be aware of what they need and try to help them get it; I can use the skill of talking to six-year-olds to make kids feel comfortable, if I have my own kid, or just when there are kids around.
_____	_____	_____
_____	_____	_____
_____	_____	_____
_____	_____	_____
_____	_____	_____
_____	_____	_____
_____	_____	_____

(continued)

Think About It (continued)

Experiences	Skills Needed or Learned	Other Ways to Use These Skills

Strengths and Skills: What's the Difference?

A strength is a natural talent you have, and it's usually something you're born with, like good eyesight. A skill is something you build from a strength. For example, somebody born with good eyesight could develop this strength into the skill of learning how to call balls and strikes as a baseball umpire.

In a nutshell, a skill is something specific that you are able to do, like call balls and strikes, build houses, or write letters. A strength is a natural ability or talent, like good eyesight, physical strength and coordination, or a way with words. Everybody has strengths. Most people have many strengths.

If you don't know what your strengths are, you may have trouble figuring out what kinds of skills you can develop. Sometimes, it is true, you don't necessarily have to have a strength in a particular area in order to develop a skill in that area. For example, if you have a great desire to learn to play guitar (which is a skill), you don't *have* to have quick fingers and a natural sense of rhythm (which are strengths). But obviously it would *help* to have these strengths. Usually, a skill is something you *build from* a strength.

So noticing our strengths is helpful in deciding what skills we want to acquire. Also, most people enjoy using their strengths and developing their strengths into skills. If, for example, you already have the strength of getting along well with people and you enjoy talking to people, then you might be quick to learn sales skills.

Define Your Strengths

Now is the time to take inventory of your strengths. Below is a list of common strengths that people can have, although it is by no means a complete list. Put a check mark next to any of the following strengths that you have. Then, on the next page, list other strengths you have that were not included in this list.

_____ Good health

_____ A strong back

_____ A good mind for numbers

_____ A good mind for words

_____ A knack for getting along with people

_____ A good memory

_____ Physical strength

_____ A knack for understanding what other people are feeling

_____ A knack for putting people at ease

_____ A knack for solving problems and figuring out puzzles

_____ An ability to learn new things fairly quickly

_____ An ability to follow directions

_____ A creative imagination

_____ Good physical reflexes

_____ Clean habits

_____ A calm nature

_____ An ability to endure physical stress

_____ An appreciation of nature and the outdoors

_____ An appreciation of animals

_____ Good self-esteem

_____ Strong family ties

What other strengths do you have? List them on the following lines:

_____

_____

_____

_____

_____

_____

_____

_____

_____

_____

_____

_____

_____

_____

Work Priorities: What's Important to You?

Below is a list of conditions that can make work pleasant and satisfying. Needless to say, you can't have them all. Think about each one, and then decide if it's very important, a little important, or not too important to you. Next to each phrase, put a "1" if it's very important, a "2" if it's a little important, or a "3" if it's not too important to you.

_____ Pleasant physical surroundings

_____ Working outdoors

_____ Working with ideas or solving problems

_____ Doing something useful

_____ Benefiting society

_____ Working with children

_____ Freedom/doing things your own way

_____ Creating new things or new ideas

_____ Variety in the work you do

_____ Directly helping other people

_____ Using your talents

_____ Creating beautiful things

_____ Getting respect

_____ Regular pay and good job benefits, such as health insurance

_____ Pleasant co-workers

_____ Chances to be promoted

_____ Involvement in key decisions

_____ Enough money to have most of the things you need and want

_____ Flexible working hours

_____ Planning work or supervising others

_____ Making a lot of money

_____ Working with people you can be friends with outside of work

_____ Physical activity on the job

_____ A routine, stable job without a lot of pressure

_____ Using your hands; working with objects

_____ Seeing the results of your work

_____ Close to where you work

_____ Chance for travel

_____ Frequent change of scenery

_____ Making your own hours

_____ Working as a member of a team

_____ Working by yourself

_____ Working for a large company

_____ Working in a small office or small company

_____ No time pressure or deadlines

See if you can pick out four or five of your "1"s that are your very most important work values. Write these phrases down on another piece of paper and keep them where you can look at them often. You will be using them as reminders as you work toward your goals.

Checkpoint

1. What is the difference between a strength and a skill?

_____

_____

_____

_____

2. What are some of your main strengths?

_____

_____

_____

_____

3. What are some of your main skills?

_____

_____

_____

_____

4. What particular working conditions are most important to you?

_____

_____

_____

_____

Chapter Two

Identify Your Experience

THE GOALS OF THIS CHAPTER ARE

❏ To remember and write down all of your work experience.

❏ To remember and write down all of your school and training history.

❏ To think about and write down all your hobbies and the things you've enjoyed doing most in your life.

❏ To remember all the different places you've been and things you've done in your life where you may have gained skills, even if you didn't realize it at the time.

Write Down Your Schooling and Training

In the spaces below, list every school you have ever attended and the courses you took.

School Worksheet

Schools	Courses
_____	_____
_____	_____
_____	_____
_____	_____
_____	_____
_____	_____
_____	_____
_____	_____
_____	_____
_____	_____
_____	_____
_____	_____
_____	_____
_____	_____
_____	_____

© JIST Works, Inc., Indianapolis, IN

In the spaces below, list any vocational courses, on-the-job training, or other training you've had. Don't forget to include the training you've had in prison. The first two lines in the table are examples to get you started.

Training Worksheet

School/Employer/Place	Courses or Training
Folsom State Prison	Eyeglass-cutting workshop; welding workshop
Sheridan Vocational School	Auto mechanics class

Work Experience

In the spaces below, list all the jobs you've ever held in your life. Be sure to include any jobs you have had in prison.

After you've listed all your jobs, list other responsibilities you've had in your life. For example, if you ever had to take care of younger brothers or sisters (or your own children), list that. If you have been responsible for managing your family's money, put that down. If you've ever been responsible for maintaining a car or any other equipment or machine, list that. If you were ever responsible for communicating information or keeping certain information private, list that.

List all the things you can think of that other people have ever depended on you for. Then see if you can list at least three skills that you had to use in order to do this job or meet this responsibility.

Job or Responsibility	Skills Used

Job or Responsibility	Skills Used

Activities and Hobbies: What Do You Like to Do?

In the spaces below, write down your favorite hobbies and spare-time activities. How have you spent your spare time in prison? What kinds of things have you missed doing while you were in prison? Include simple things like walking, reading, and visiting friends, as well as more complicated things like working on cars, photography, or traveling.

_____

_____

_____

_____

_____

_____

_____

_____

_____

_____

_____

_____

What Else?

What else have you done in your life? What other accomplishments have you achieved? What other tasks have you performed?

Have you ever painted a room? Have you ever driven a long distance in a short period of time? Have you ever fixed anything? Have you ever solved a problem for someone else?

Have you ever taught yourself how to do something? Has someone else ever taught you to do something, other than in school? Have you ever used a special tool, like a soldering iron or a jackhammer?

Have you ever researched the answer to a question? Have you ever won an award? Have you ever been recognized for doing something well?

Write down every accomplishment you can think of that you haven't already written. They don't have to be fancy—just accomplishments that you were proud of.

_____

_____

_____

_____

_____

_____

_____

_____

_____

Checkpoint

1. What have been some of your most important school or training experiences?

   _____

   _____

   _____

   _____

2. What has been your most important work experience?

   _____

   _____

   _____

   _____

3. What are some achievements you've accomplished in your life?

   _____

   _____

   _____

   _____

4. What responsibilities have you fulfilled in your life?

   _____

   _____

   _____

   _____

Chapter Three

Identify Your Skills

THE GOALS OF THIS CHAPTER ARE

❏ To learn to break your major skills down into several smaller skills.

❏ To take a complete inventory of your skills, including major ones and smaller ones.

❏ To determine what skills you'd like to use most in the future, and what skills you'd like to gain or improve.

Break Down Your Skills

Most activities require sets of skills that can be broken down into smaller skills. For example, here are some (but not all) of the skills needed to drive a car:

- ❏ Reading road signs

- ❏ Having good hand-to-eye coordination

- ❏ Parallel parking

- ❏ Putting on the brakes and accelerating correctly in different situations

- ❏ Responding rapidly to other cars' brake lights

- ❏ Adapting to any changing conditions of the road or in traffic

- ❏ Understanding road maps and directions

- ❏ Concentrating

- ❏ Backing up

- ❏ Avoiding dangerous situations

- ❏ Having patience in heavy traffic

- ❏ Using turn signals

- ❏ Interpreting information from rear-view mirrors

When you break down activities into sets of skills, you can see that most activities are more complicated than they look at first glance. Most activities require you to be able to do more than just one thing.

Looking at your skills this way, you get a sense of how many different things you are able to do.

Think About It

On the lines below, list three skills you have, and then break each skill down into at least three smaller skills.

Major Skill	Smaller Skills
_____	_____
	_____
	_____
	_____
	_____
_____	_____
	_____
	_____
	_____
	_____
_____	_____
	_____
	_____
	_____
	_____

Different Types of Skills

There are different types of skills. In general, your skills can be divided into three categories:

❏ **Specific job skills.** These are skills you learn while on a job. These are also sometimes simply called *job-related skills.* They include skills such as truck driving and landscaping.

❏ **General job skills.** These are skills that can apply to many different kinds of jobs. These are skills such as keeping track of money or supervising a team. These are also sometimes called *transferable skills* because you can use them when you transfer from one job to another.

❏ **Personality skills.** These are also sometimes called *adaptive skills,* or self-management skills. You use these skills all the time, to get along with people and to run your life. Patience and tolerance are two of these skills.

The skills you use most of the time are the personality skills. Though job skills are also very important, personality skills are the most basic. You need them in every situation, including work.

Your Personality Skills

On the following lines, list three things about yourself that help you get along in life or that make you a "good" person. Take your time.

1. _____

2. _____

3. _____

These three traits may be some of the most important things you need to know about yourself. They define the way you see yourself and what you have to offer others. Mentioning these traits in a job interview may get you hired over someone who actually has more experience than you do.

Identify Your Personality Skills and General Skills

The following sections will help you figure out the personality and general skills that you have now, as well as ones you would like to gain or improve.

Personality Skills Worksheet

The worksheet that follows contains a list of personality skills. The first group of skills—"Basic Personality Skills"—is the most important one. Many employers will not hire an applicant who does not have these skills. The second group of skills is important for many jobs.

Directions: Look over the list and put a check mark beside any skill that you feel you have now. In the "Want to Improve" column, put a check mark beside any skill that you feel you need to improve. (Later in this book we will go over ways to develop and improve your skills.)

At the end of the worksheet, you can add other skills that you feel you have now or want to improve that are not listed here.

Personality Skills Worksheet

Basic Personality Skills

Skill	Have Now	Want to Improve
Good attendance		
Honesty		
Arriving on time		
Following instructions		
Meeting deadlines		
Hard working		
Getting along with others		

Other Personality Skills

Skill	Have Now	Want to Improve
Ambition		
Patience		
Flexibility		
Maturity		
Assertiveness		
Dependability		
Learning quickly		
Completing assignments		

Other Personality Skills

Skill	Have Now	Want to Improve
Sincerity		
Motivation		
Problem-solving ability		
Friendliness		
Sense of humor		
Leadership		
Physical stamina		
Enthusiasm		
Good sense of direction		
Persistence		
Self-motivation		
Accepting responsibility		
Results-oriented		
Willing to ask questions		
Pride in doing a good job		
Willing to learn		
Creative		

(continued)

Personality Skills Worksheet (continued)

More Personality Skills (Add your own)		
Skill	**Have Now**	**Want to Improve**

Your Top Personality Skills

Review your list of personality skills. Then, in the spaces below, list the three personality skills that you feel are most important for an employer to know about you.

1. _____

2. _____

3. _____

Personality Skills to Improve

Now list the three personality skills that you feel are the most important ones for you to work on improving. (Keep these in mind for later. We'll work on improving skills in a later chapter.)

1. _____

2. _____

3. _____

Your General Job Skills

Personality skills are more like "who you are," while general job skills, like being organized, are "things you do." Many skills, like "accept responsibility," could be put into either group. Don't worry about this in making your lists. There is some overlap, and it just isn't that important to worry about.

Remember:
- Personality skills are more like "who you are."
- General job skills are "things you do."
- Some skills can go into either group.

On the lines below, list three of your general job skills. Remember, these are the skills that you can take with you from job to job. It is important for you to know these skills so you can share them with a potential employer.

1. _____

2. _____

3. _____

There are hundreds of general job skills. The worksheet that follows includes the ones that are most important to employers. Are the skills you listed included on the worksheet?

General Job Skills Worksheet

The skills on this worksheet are organized into clusters. This is to help you identify major types of jobs that will suit you best.

Directions: Read the list and put a check mark beside each skill that you feel you are strong in. Then go through the list again and put another check mark in the "Use in Next Job" column if you think you want to use that skill in your next job.

Note: Jobs that tend to pay more or have more responsibility often require one or more of the "key" skills at the beginning of the worksheet. If you have any of these skills, you will want to emphasize them to potential employers.

General Job Skills Worksheet

Key General Job Skills (These are very important to employers)		
Skill	**Already Strong**	**Use in Next Job**
Meeting deadlines		
Planning		
Public speaking		
Budgeting and money management		

Key General Job Skills (These are very important to employers)

Skill	Already Strong	Use in Next Job
Supervising others		
Instructing others		
Accepting responsibility		
Managing people		
Meeting the public		
Working effectively in a group		
Organizing projects		
Taking risks		
Self-controlling		
Self-motivating		
Detail oriented		
Knowledge of basic computer skills		
Explaining things to others		
Problem solving		
Good writing skills		
Good math skills		

General Job Skills Worksheet (continued)

Other General Job Skills: Working with Things

Skill	Already Strong	Use in Next Job
Using my hands		
Assembling things		
Building things		
Constructing, repairing buildings		
Making things		
Observing, inspecting things		
Driving, operating vehicles		
Operating tools and machinery		
Using complex equipment		

Other General Job Skills: Working with Data

Skill	Already Strong	Use in Next Job
Analyzing data, facts		
Auditing records		
Investigating		
Using the Internet		
Sending and receiving e-mail		

Other General Job Skills: Working with Data

Skill	Already Strong	Use in Next Job
Researching and locating information		
Calculating, computing		
Classifying data		
Counting		
Observing		

Other General Job Skills: Working with People

Skill	Already Strong	Use in Next Job
Patient		
Sensitive		
Social		
Tactful		
Teaching		
Interviewing others		
Listening		
Tolerant		
Understanding		

(continued)

General Job Skills Worksheet *(continued)*

Other General Job Skills: Working with People

Skill	Already Strong	Use in Next Job
Kind		
Diplomatic		
Counseling people		
Confronting (when necessary)		
Trusting		
Can be firm		

Other General Job Skills: Using Words and Ideas

Skill	Already Strong	Use in Next Job
Can be logical		
Speaking in public		
Designing		
Editing		
Remembering information		
Writing clearly		
Corresponding with others		
Creative		

Other General Job Skills: Using Leadership Ability

Skill	Already Strong	Use in Next Job
Arranging social functions		
Competitive		
Motivating people		
Can be decisive		
Running meetings		
Delegating		
Working out agreements		
Planning		

Other General Job Skills: Using Creative, Artistic Ability

Skill	Already Strong	Use in Next Job
Dancing, body movement		
Drawing, art		
Performing, acting		
Playing instruments		
Presenting artistic ideas		
Music appreciation		
Expressive		

(continued)

General Job Skills Worksheet (continued)

Other General Job Skills: Add Your Own

Skill	Already Strong	Use in Next Job

Your Top General Job Skills

Review your worksheet of general job skills. List the five that you are best in or that are most important to you.

1. _____

2. _____

3. _____

4. _____

5. _____

General Job Skills to Improve

Now list the five skills you most want to improve. (We'll work on improving your skills later in this book.)

1. _____

2. _____

3. _____

4. _____

5. _____

In the next chapter, you will create an "inventory" of your experiences. This listing of experiences can be used to help you uncover even more skills, including specific job skills.

Checkpoint

1. What are personality skills?

   _____

   _____

   _____

2. What are general job skills?

   _____

   _____

   _____

(continued)

Checkpoint (continued)

_____

_____

3. Why is it so important for you to know and be able to communicate your personality and general job skills?

_____

_____

_____

_____

_____

_____

_____

_____

Think About It

Look back at the three top personality skills that you listed. Think about situations in your life when you used each of those skills. Briefly describe those situations and how you used the skills. Can you support your claim that you have these skills? (This becomes very important during job interviews.)

Personality Skill 1

_____

_____

_____

How I used this skill:

_____

_____

_____

_____

Personality Skill 2

_____

_____

_____

How I used this skill:

_____

_____

_____

_____

(continued)

Think About It (continued)

Personality Skill 3

_____

_____

_____

How I used this skill:

_____

_____

_____

_____

General Job Skill 1

_____

_____

_____

How I used this skill:

_____

_____

_____

_____

General Job Skill 2

_____

_____

_____

How I used this skill:

_____

_____

_____

_____

General Job Skill 3

_____

_____

_____

How I used this skill:

_____

_____

_____

_____

Take Inventory of Your Skills

In chapter 2, you listed experiences you've had in your life that could have contributed to the number of skills you now have. In this chapter, you have seen how many different smaller skills you need to perform big tasks, and you have gotten an idea of how many skills you already have.

On the next pages, you will look again at your work, school, training, and hobby experience. But this time you will look at them with an eye toward identifying skills that you strengthened or gained in each of these experiences.

Skills Inventory Worksheet

Directions: Complete the worksheet that follows to target the key experiences and skills you gained through education, work, volunteer activities, and other experiences.

The worksheet asks you to list in the left column things you studied or did, and in the right column, skills you strengthened or gained as a result. For example, one young man listed his literature class on the left. On the right, he noted:

"Helped me to be able to write letters, read documents, and fill out forms better, like applications."

Education and Training

Junior High School

On the lines below, list your junior high school coursework and the skills you gained.

Subjects Studied	Skills Strengthened or Gained

On the lines below, include any special organizations that you participated in, whether in or out of school. These might be clubs, teams, hobby groups, and so on.

Extracurricular Activities	Skills Strengthened or Gained

(continued)

Education and Training *(continued)*

High School

On the lines below, list your high school coursework and the skills you gained.

Subjects Studied	Skills Strengthened or Gained

On the lines below, include any special organizations that you participated in, whether in or out of school. These might be clubs, teams, hobby groups, and so on.

Extracurricular Activities	Skills Strengthened or Gained

After High School

In this section, list any education or training you had after high school. Include training you have received in the military, if any.

Subjects Studied	Skills Strengthened or Gained

In this section, list activities and organizations that you participated in.

Extracurricular Activities	Skills Strengthened or Gained

(continued)

Work History

For this section, you will list all the jobs you've had and what your responsibilities were. In the right column, list the skills you strengthened or gained. Include part-time jobs, summer jobs, or self-employment like mowing lawns or baby-sitting.

Job and Responsibilities	Skills Strengthened or Gained

Job and Responsibilities	Skills Strengthened or Gained

Job and Responsibilities	Skills Strengthened or Gained

Job and Responsibilities	Skills Strengthened or Gained

Volunteer Experience

You don't have to have been paid for work to have valuable work experience. In this section, list any volunteer work you have done, and the skills you strengthened or gained while doing it.

Volunteer Job and Responsibilities	Skills Strengthened or Gained

Volunteer Job and Responsibilities	Skills Strengthened or Gained

(continued)

Volunteer Experience (continued)

Volunteer Job and Responsibilities	Skills Strengthened or Gained

Hobbies, Leisure Activities, and Other Life Experiences

For this section, list hobbies, interests, family activities, or any other activities that have led you to develop specific skills. Take plenty of time to think and remember. As we said earlier in this book, you have many more skills than you realize!

For example, maybe you helped take care of the younger children in your family. Doing this would help you gain skills in child care, patience, taking responsibility, food preparation, and other areas.

If you like to use a computer, you may have gained skills in using the Internet to find information, keyboarding and word processing, or Web page design.

Activity	Skills Strengthened or Gained

Activity	Skills Strengthened or Gained

Activity	Skills Strengthened or Gained

Activity	Skills Strengthened or Gained

(continued)

Hobbies, Leisure Activities, and Other Life Experiences *(continued)*

Your Top Skills

Now you will need to go back over the entire worksheet you just completed. Use each section to complete the lists that follow here.

Things I Do Best

1. _____
2. _____
3. _____
4. _____
5. _____

Skills I Most Enjoy Using

1. _____
2. _____
3. _____
4. _____
5. _____

Skills I Most Want to Improve

1. _____
2. _____
3. _____
4. _____
5. _____

Skills I Want to Use in My Next Job

1. _____
2. _____
3. _____
4. _____
5. _____

Congratulations! You now have an inventory to help you make valuable decisions about your life and your work.

Don't worry about figuring out your entire life goals right now. People grow and change throughout their lives, and you are bound to change, too. You can't predict the future. So make the decisions that make sense now. That's the best anyone can do.

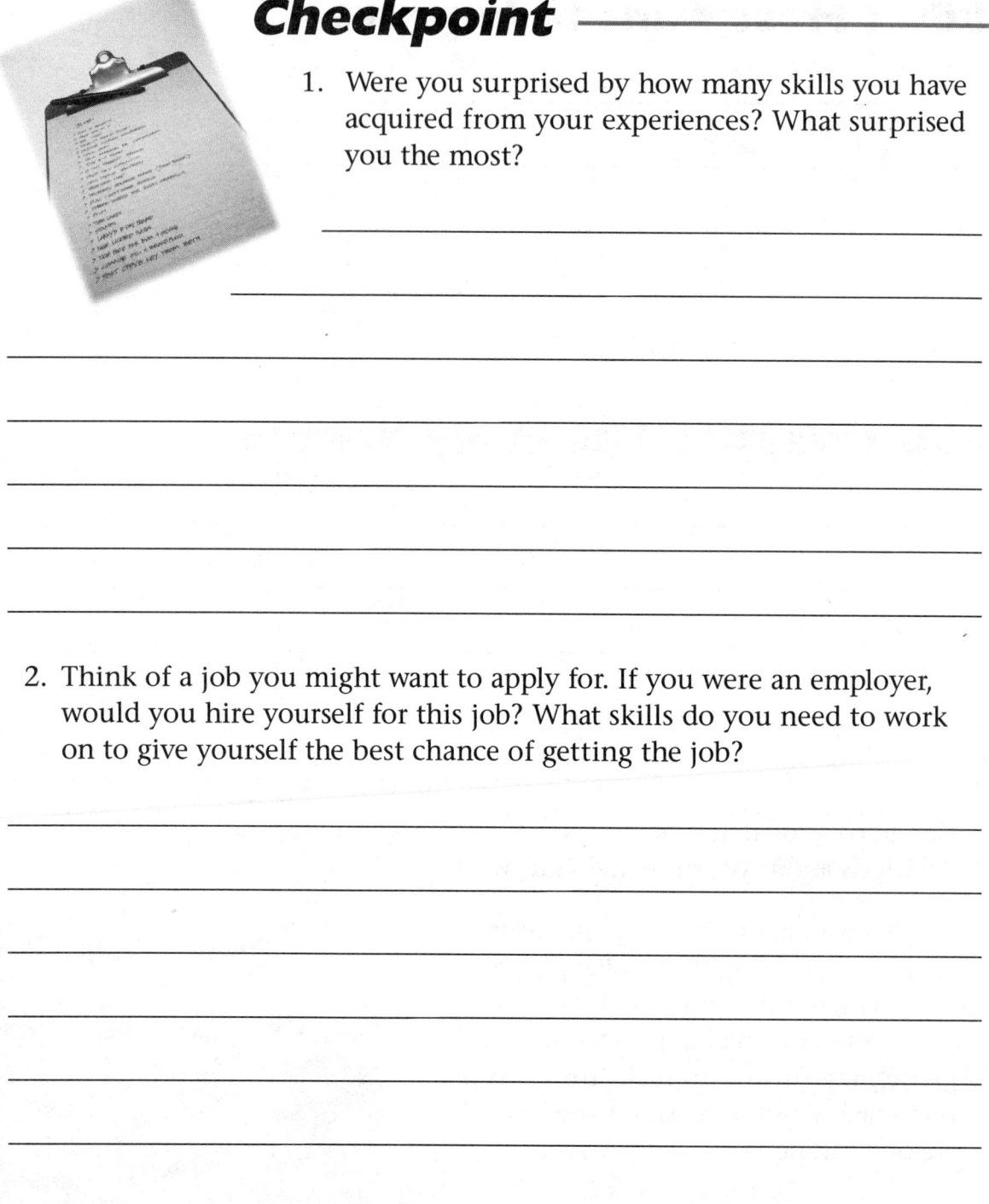

Checkpoint

1. Were you surprised by how many skills you have acquired from your experiences? What surprised you the most?

    _____

    _____

    _____

    _____

    _____

2. Think of a job you might want to apply for. If you were an employer, would you hire yourself for this job? What skills do you need to work on to give yourself the best chance of getting the job?

    _____

    _____

    _____

    _____

    _____

    _____

    _____

Chapter Four

Put It All into Action

THE GOALS OF THIS CHAPTER ARE

❏ To start thinking about what kind of career you'd like to have.

❏ To learn where to look for information about careers.

❏ To realize that sometimes it's worth passing up small pleasures to achieve long-term goals.

❏ To improve your skills through training and education.

❏ To start setting concrete job and career–related goals for yourself.

The Right Job for You

The happiest job in the world for you is one where you will be able to express your real self, your natural interests, your strengths, your mental and physical abilities, and your personality—and also serve your community and your world.

Many people let others tell them what their possibilities are, what their strengths are, and what their purpose in life is. That's why eight out of ten people are unhappy with their work. How does this happen? People choose their careers without thinking, without doing the "fieldwork" of discovering themselves first. Or sometimes people grab at whatever work they can get.

If, before you went to prison, you had work that was not satisfying and did not pay you enough, you may have felt that crime was an easy solution to avoiding a life of hardship. But now you know that crime is no solution at all.

Career planning—exploring other jobs or careers that may be a better fit for you—is the *real* solution. But career planning takes effort and commitment. It is a *job* in and of itself. But the rewards are enormous. Career planning is yet another way of discovering yourself—and of creating the life you really want for yourself.

Start to Think About Careers

Finding the right career takes time, energy, and often money for training or counseling. But it's worth it if you can get the job that pays what you need, develops your potential, and uses the skills and talents you have enjoyed using your whole life.

If you enjoy working with your hands, using tools, and fixing things, a few jobs that you might consider are automotive mechanic, machinist, musical instrument repairer/tuner, and water treatment plant operator. All of these jobs require some training. But some companies are willing to train you as you work for them. All of these occupations offer good working conditions, good pay, and a lot of independence on the job.

Or you may want to develop a trade related to construction, such as carpenter, bricklayer, plasterer, or roofer. These trades require some training. But there are many jobs available, pay is good, and the work is generally outside. If you enjoy being outdoors, you might also consider forestry, logging, house painting, and landscape gardening. Or you could be a mail carrier.

If you like being on the road instead of in just one place, you could be a bus driver, taxi driver, truck driver, subway operator, or even a railroad transportation worker (which requires some training). Opportunities are good in all of these fields, and working conditions are not bad (if you don't mind heavy traffic sometimes!).

If you want to work in a sales- or marketing-related profession, you could become a travel agent, real estate broker, insurance agent, or a retail sales worker.

If you are creative and you like to look closely at things, you could be a photographer or a graphic designer. If you enjoy being in libraries, you could become a library clerk or an archivist. If you like working with numbers, you could be a bookkeeper.

See the last pages in this book for a list of jobs that are available for people without a college degree.

Jobs That Match Your Skills

There are thousands of job titles. Yet your task is to select just a few jobs that best fit your skills and interests. One way to do this is to consider groups of similar jobs.

The list below provides groups of jobs organized into 12 major clusters of interest areas. Later, you can go to a library and look up the jobs in the clusters. For now, just check the clusters of jobs that sound most interesting to you.

____ **01 Artistic**. An interest in the creative expression of feelings or ideas.

____ **02 Scientific**. An interest in discovering, collecting, and analyzing information about the natural world, and in applying scientific research findings to problems in medicine and the natural sciences.

_____ **03 Plants and Animals.** An interest in working with plants and animals, usually outdoors.

_____ **04 Protective.** An interest in using authority to protect people and property.

_____ **05 Mechanical.** An interest in applying mechanical principles to practical situations by use of machines or hand tools.

_____ **06 Industrial.** An interest in repetitive, concrete, organized activities done in an industrial or factory setting.

_____ **07 Business Detail.** An interest in organized, clearly defined activities requiring accuracy and attention to details, primarily in an office setting.

_____ **08 Selling.** An interest in bringing others to a particular point of view by personal persuasion, using sales and promotional techniques.

_____ **09 Accommodating.** An interest in catering to the wishes and needs of others, usually on a one-on-one basis.

_____ **10 Humanitarian.** An interest in helping others with their mental, spiritual, social, physical, or vocational needs.

_____ **11 Leading-Influencing.** An interest in leading and influencing others by using high-level verbal or numerical abilities.

_____ **12 Physical Performing.** An interest in physical activities performed before an audience.

Gather Information

You will probably need more information to identify the jobs that interest you. You need to know about required skills and needed training or education. There may be jobs that match your skills and interests that you haven't thought of yet.

Here are some ways to find out more about the jobs that interest you.

1. Visit the library. A larger library will have many resources on education and training options and other career topics. Ask your librarian for help in finding what you need. You may find the following publications particularly useful:

   ■ *Occupational Outlook Handbook:* Published by the U.S. Department of Labor and JIST, this book provides good descriptions of the top few hundred jobs in this country. It includes information on the nature of work, average pay rates, education and training required, projections for growth, and many other details.

   ■ *Young Person's Occupational Outlook Handbook*: Covers all the jobs in the *Occupational Outlook Handbook* in an easy-to-understand format.

   ■ *Exploring Careers:* Written for young people, this book describes jobs in major clusters, featuring people who actually work in the jobs in some of the descriptions.

   ■ The *Guide for Occupational Exploration:* Provides details on the 12 interest areas and the many jobs available within them.

2. Talk to people who already have jobs in your field of interest. Contact employers and make an appointment or ask questions over the telephone about what skills and training you would need in order for them to hire you. Talk to a guidance counselor at a high school, vocational or technical school, or college or university about the types of jobs you are interested in.

3. If you know how to use the Internet, a lot of information is available there. There are some great Web sites to help young people plan their education, training, career, and life. The *Occupational Outlook Handbook* lists some Internet sites, and you can get career information and links to other sites by visiting www.jist.com, the site that belongs to JIST Publishing, the publisher of this book and many other books about job seeking.

   The major Internet service providers, such as America Online, can help you find links to good sites. Or you can use a search engine like Infoseek.com or Yahoo.com to find other sites on topics that interest you.

Keep an Open Mind

As you are gathering information about different jobs, keep an open mind and pay attention to ideas that come your way. Read the want ads. Watch TV, read books about different jobs, talk to counselors, and talk to people in various fields of work.

Think About It

When you are ready, on the lines below, make a list of five to ten occupations that might interest you.

1. _____
2. _____
3. _____
4. _____
5. _____
6. _____
7. _____
8. _____
9. _____
10. _____

For each occupation you listed, research the answers to the questions on the next page. But be prepared; this research will require lots of time and effort. It will probably take months, maybe even a year or more. You may need to call companies, make appointments, and be "referred" from one person to the next. Sooner or later, though, you will come across helpful people who can answer your questions.

Arrange conversations and interviews with successful people in your chosen field or fields. It may be uncomfortable to approach people and ask for their time, but just remember that people enjoy talking about themselves and what they do.

Job Information Worksheet

Name of job or career field: _____

How do you enter into this field? _____

_____

What would be an entry-level (starting) position and how much would it pay?

_____

How much can you expect to make after you've been in this field for a few years?

_____ Ten years? _____

Is there a good future in this field? _____

Does the job offer security? _____

Do you think you will be happy with the working conditions? Why or why not?

_____

_____

Are there enough job openings in this field? _____

Can you get work in this field through employment agencies or temp work agencies?

_____

What strengths and skills are needed for this kind of work? _____

_____

_____

_____

What kind of preparation, experience, or training is required for this kind of work?

_____

_____

(continued)

Job Information Worksheet *(continued)*

Do you have the right education and experience to enter this field? _____

If not, how can you get it? _____

_____

_____

Will this work let you live where you want to live? _____

Will this work hurt your physical or emotional health in any way? If so, how? _____

_____

_____

_____

What purpose does this work serve for society? _____

_____

_____

How does this work fit in with your own sense of meaning and purpose in life? _____

_____

_____

Job Information Worksheet

Name of job or career field: _____

How do you enter into this field? _____

_____

What would be an entry-level (starting) position and how much would it pay?

_____

How much can you expect to make after you've been in this field for a few years?

_____ Ten years? _____

Is there a good future in this field? _____

Does the job offer security? _____

Do you think you will be happy with the working conditions? Why or why not?

_____

_____

Are there enough job openings in this field? _____

Can you get work in this field through employment agencies or temp work agencies?

_____

What strengths and skills are needed for this kind of work? _____

_____

_____

_____

What kind of preparation, experience, or training is required for this kind of work?

_____

_____

(continued)

Job Information Worksheet (continued)

Do you have the right education and experience to enter this field? _____

If not, how can you get it? _____

_____

_____

Will this work let you live where you want to live? _____

Will this work hurt your physical or emotional health in any way? If so, how? _____

_____

_____

_____

What purpose does this work serve for society? _____

_____

_____

How does this work fit in with your own sense of meaning and purpose in life? _____

_____

_____

Job Information Worksheet

Name of job or career field: _____

How do you enter into this field? _____

_____

What would be an entry-level (starting) position and how much would it pay?

_____

How much can you expect to make after you've been in this field for a few years?

_____ Ten years? _____

Is there a good future in this field? _____

Does the job offer security? _____

Do you think you will be happy with the working conditions? Why or why not?

_____

_____

Are there enough job openings in this field? _____

Can you get work in this field through employment agencies or temp work agencies?

_____

What strengths and skills are needed for this kind of work? _____

_____

_____

_____

What kind of preparation, experience, or training is required for this kind of work?

_____

_____

(continued)

Job Information Worksheet (continued)

Do you have the right education and experience to enter this field? _____

If not, how can you get it? _____

_____

_____

Will this work let you live where you want to live? _____

Will this work hurt your physical or emotional health in any way? If so, how? _____

_____

_____

_____

What purpose does this work serve for society? _____

_____

_____

How does this work fit in with your own sense of meaning and purpose in life? _____

_____

_____

Job Information Worksheet

Name of job or career field: _____

How do you enter into this field? _____

_____

What would be an entry-level (starting) position and how much would it pay?

_____

How much can you expect to make after you've been in this field for a few years?

_____ Ten years? _____

Is there a good future in this field? _____

Does the job offer security? _____

Do you think you will be happy with the working conditions? Why or why not?

_____

_____

Are there enough job openings in this field? _____

Can you get work in this field through employment agencies or temp work agencies?

_____

What strengths and skills are needed for this kind of work? _____

_____

_____

_____

What kind of preparation, experience, or training is required for this kind of work?

_____

_____

(continued)

Job Information Worksheet (continued)

Do you have the right education and experience to enter this field? _____

If not, how can you get it? _____

_____

_____

Will this work let you live where you want to live? _____

Will this work hurt your physical or emotional health in any way? If so, how? _____

_____

_____

_____

What purpose does this work serve for society? _____

_____

_____

How does this work fit in with your own sense of meaning and purpose in life? _____

_____

_____

Job Information Worksheet

Name of job or career field: _____

How do you enter into this field? _____

_____

What would be an entry-level (starting) position and how much would it pay?

_____

How much can you expect to make after you've been in this field for a few years?

_____ Ten years? _____

Is there a good future in this field? _____

Does the job offer security? _____

Do you think you will be happy with the working conditions? Why or why not?

_____

_____

Are there enough job openings in this field? _____

Can you get work in this field through employment agencies or temp work agencies?

_____

What strengths and skills are needed for this kind of work? _____

_____

_____

_____

What kind of preparation, experience, or training is required for this kind of work?

_____

_____

(continued)

Job Information Worksheet (continued)

Do you have the right education and experience to enter this field? _____

If not, how can you get it? _____

_____

_____

Will this work let you live where you want to live? _____

Will this work hurt your physical or emotional health in any way? If so, how? _____

_____

_____

_____

What purpose does this work serve for society? _____

_____

_____

How does this work fit in with your own sense of meaning and purpose in life? _____

_____

_____

Training Now Will Pay Off Later

It is natural, but not usually a good idea, to seek instant gratification—to grab at something that makes you feel a little bit better right now instead of waiting for something much better that could come later.

You may have a chance, at some point, to get trained in some skill, or to learn a trade. Training takes time, and you often get paid little or nothing during that time. Taking courses at a trade school might even cost you some money. But it's worth it in the end: Your salary will be higher than the minimum-wage jobs you can get without training. And you can take more pride in the work you do.

Take the long view. Where do you want to be five years from now? How much money do you want to be earning? What kind of work do you want to be doing?

Often, landing the right job is a matter of delaying gratification long enough to get qualified. It's worth it.

Put in a little extra time and energy now, and you will be that much happier later. It really works like that.

The following pages describe some of your options for gaining skills that can put you on a career track.

Formal Schooling

One option for gaining new skills or improving your skills is, of course, to go to school. There are many types of schools, such as colleges, universities, vocational schools, and technical schools. If you are thinking about entering a school program, here are some things to consider:

What Type of School Will Provide the Training You Need?

Some options are as follows:

- High school career training programs

- Community and junior colleges

- Four-year colleges and universities

- Vocational and technical schools

How Will You Pay for It?

Some options might be the following:

- Financial aid through the school or a government program

- Help from relatives or your employer

- Earning enough money by working while you go through the program

- Earn a scholarship

The Military

Another option for receiving training is the armed forces. You can enlist in the service and learn job skills that you can use for a civilian job when you have finished your tour of duty.

You can also qualify for scholarships and other forms of financial aid for career training programs and even university degrees.

Local recruitment offices can help you find information about career possibilities through the military. There are books such as *Military Careers* that are put out by the U.S. government.

These books contain information about available programs. Ask a librarian to help you find this information.

On-the-Job Training

Some jobs do not require any formal training before you take the job. You learn by doing. This kind of job training can last from a few days to several years.

Your employer might put you under the supervision of another worker or send you to classes to train for the job.

You might also work toward a job you want in a business or organization by starting in an entry-level job. An entry-level job is often low skilled and low paying, but you can learn about the job you want to move up to. You can learn much about the organization and receive promotions if you do your work well.

Apprenticeships

An apprentice learns a trade by combining on-the-job training with classroom instruction. The program can last from one to six years.

Most programs are put on by employers, government agencies, and labor unions. Bricklayers, auto mechanics, carpenters, and electricians are trade workers who learn their skills through an apprentice program.

Improve Your General Skills

Remember that general (transferable) job skills are ones that you can use in a variety of different jobs. Now that you've done some career planning and exploration, maybe you can see that there are certain general skills you will need to pick up or improve in order to have the kind of career you're aiming for.

Think About It

On the lines below, list some general (transferable) skills that you might like to acquire or improve.

_____

_____

_____

_____

_____

_____

_____

_____

Resources for Learning General Skills

You could ask for help from a friend or relative who is good at the skill you want to learn.

Also, you can find out about community programs in your area. High schools, hospitals, libraries, state universities, and many other organizations offer a wide range of adult programs on evenings and weekends. The cost is usually low. These programs cover both personal and practical skills. Some topics covered in the courses could include math skills, reading skills, computers, and assertiveness.

Career Research Pointers

Finding the right career takes time, energy, and often money for training or counseling. But it is well worth it, to get the job that pays what you need, develops your potential, and uses the skills and talents you have enjoyed using your whole life.

Arrange conversations and interviews with successful people in your chosen field or fields. But do not take anyone's word that a certain job market is "tight"—not many jobs are available—until you've researched it carefully. Talk to a lot of people about it, and read up on it. Job markets change often; a tight market today could be an open market tomorrow.

Remember: The happiest job in the world for you is in the career field where you can best express yourself—your natural interests, strengths, skills, and character—while serving your values and your purpose in life. However, the job you get today may not be the one you want to keep for a lifetime. It's good to have different types of goals for yourself.

Short-Term and Long-Term Goals

You need short-term goals and long-term goals. A short-term goal might be a job that you can get fairly quickly, that will help you to survive, even though you won't want to stick with it for years and years. A long-term goal might be your ideal job, but that might require training, time, experience, contacts, etc.

A few questions that may help you set your short-term goals are

■ Where do I want to go, and when do I want to get there?

- Who can help me? (teachers, counselors, family, friends, placement officers, librarians, etc.)

- What goals must I achieve first, before I achieve all of my lifetime goals?

- What obstacles might come between me and my goals? How will I get past them?

Write down three long-term goals and three short-term goals.

Long-term goal #1: _____

_____

Long-term goal #2: _____

_____

Long-term goal #3: _____

_____

Short-term goal #1: _____

_____

Short-term goal #2: _____

_____

Short-term goal #3: _____

_____

Keep Your Goals Realistic and Manageable

It is important to keep your goals realistic. The way to do this is to break goals down into steps. Here's an example:

Goal: Taking a math class

Mini-Goals:

■ Finding out where and when the right class is offered.

■ Finding out how much the class costs.

■ Registering for the class.

■ Buying the books for the class.

Worksheets: Make Your Goals More Manageable

Take every goal you wrote down on the previous page and break it down into at least five "mini-goals."

Goal-Management Worksheet

Goal	Mini-Goals
	1.
	2.
	3.
	4.
	5.
	1.
	2.
	3.
	4.
	5.

(continued)

Goal-Management Worksheet (continued)

Goal	Mini-Goals
	1.
	2.
	3.
	4.
	5.
	1.
	2.
	3.
	4.
	5.
	1.
	2.
	3.
	4.
	5.
	1.
	2.
	3.
	4.
	5.

Action Plans

An action plan is a complete step-by-step process for accomplishing a goal. Everything you need to do to meet your goal has to go into the action plan, including

- Information or training you must get

- Books you must read

- Studying and researching you need to do

- People you must contact

- Places you must go

- The resume you must write

- Applications you must fill out

You should also have back-up plans. Things often take longer than you think they will, or they don't turn out exactly according to plan. Have alternatives in mind, and be ready to bounce back when things don't go quite right. It's okay to change your plan according to the circumstances.

Look at your short-term and long-term goals. Now that you know some of the "mini-goals," you can start writing complete action plans:

Goal: Learn to type

Action Plan: Go to the library and get lists of schools and community colleges in my area. Call schools and see if any offer typing classes. Find out when the typing classes are and how much they cost. Register for a class. Make time to practice typing.

Possible Back-Up Plans: If there are no typing classes in my area, or if I can't afford them, go back to the library and see if there are any books that teach typing. Check in the library for audiotapes that teach typing. Check in the bookstores for audiotapes or books that teach typing. See if any of my friends who type can teach me to type or recommend someplace to learn typing.

Action Plan Worksheets

Goal

Action Plan	Back-Up Plan

Goal

Action Plan	Back-Up Plan

(continued)

(continued)

Goal	
Action Plan	**Back-Up Plan**

Goal	
Action Plan	**Back-Up Plan**

(continued)

(continued)

Goal	
Action Plan	**Back-Up Plan**

Goal

Action Plan	Back-Up Plan

Daily Action Plans

You can only work toward your goals one day at time.

Do something every day, no matter how small, to work toward your goals. Imagine yourself accomplishing the goals you've set for yourself—one, two, three, five, or even ten years from now! Make sure that you can really see your goals in your mind.

It's a good idea to write an action plan for each day. Look at your goals and ask yourself, "What can I reasonably hope to accomplish today that will help bring me closer to my goals?"

Daily Planning Worksheet

Date	Things to Do	Time Required

Date	Things to Do	Time Required

Final Words About Goals

You have a better chance of reaching any goal if you:

- Make the goal very specific.

- Decide on a plan to reach the goal.

- Gather any information you need.

- Keep track of your progress.

- Find someone to be supportive and give you encouragement along the way.

- Stick with your plan and do it!

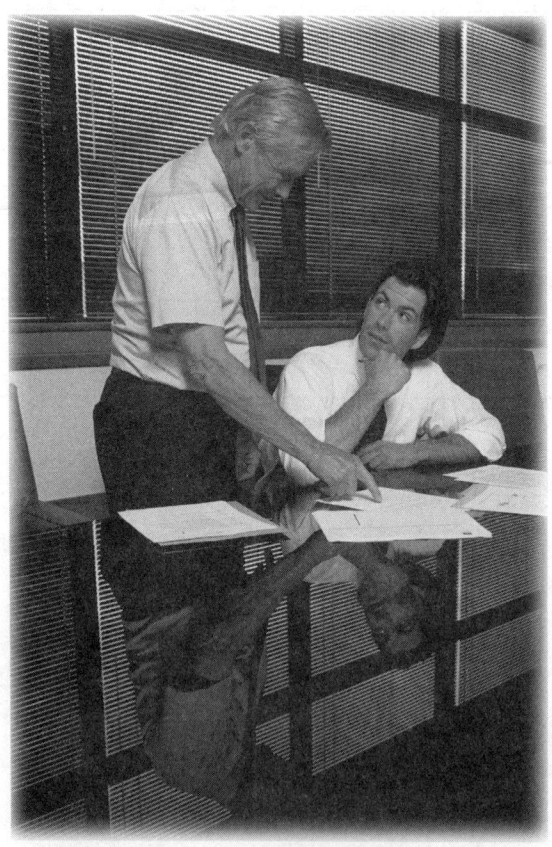

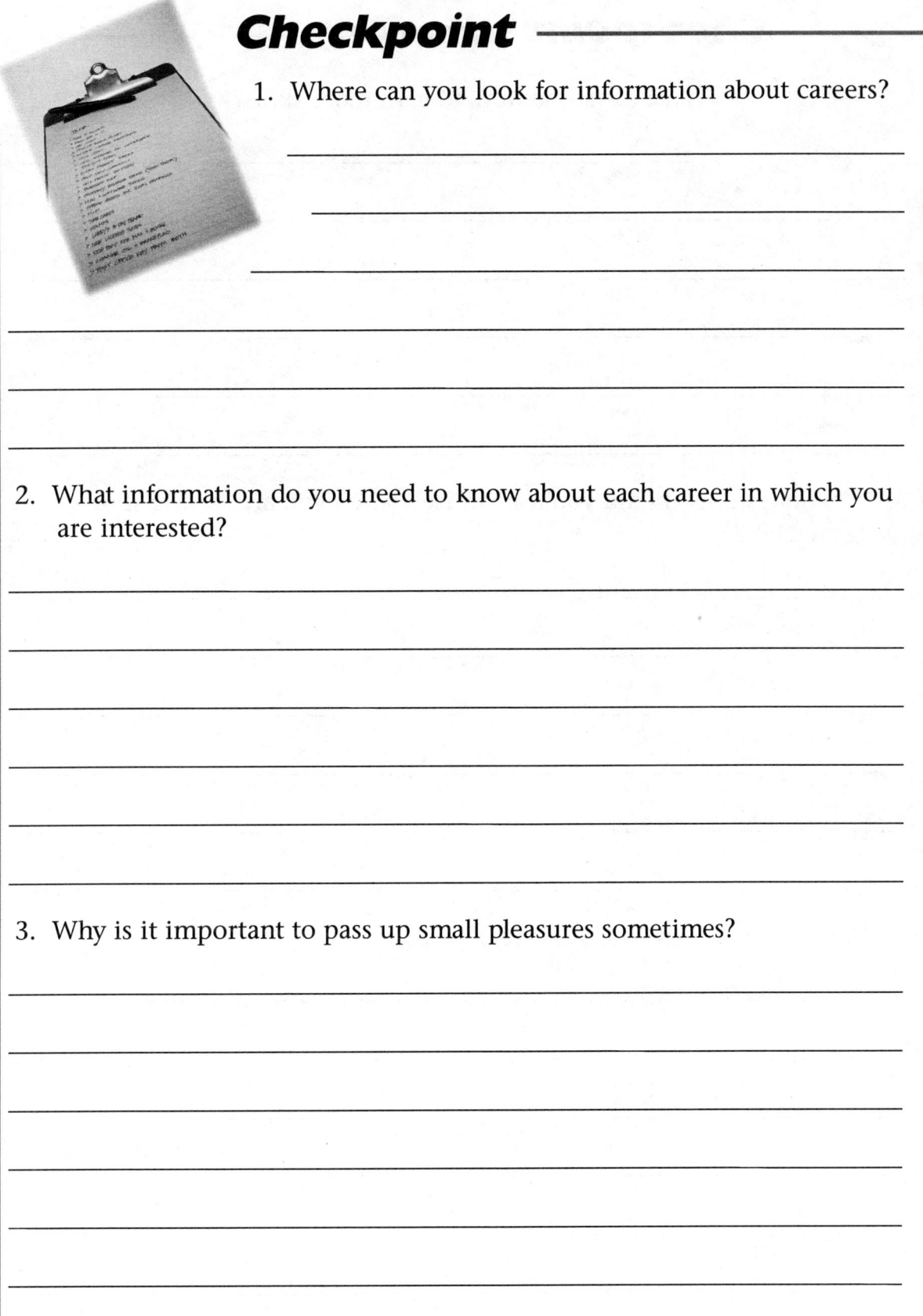

Checkpoint

1. Where can you look for information about careers?

_____

_____

_____

_____

_____

_____

2. What information do you need to know about each career in which you are interested?

_____

_____

_____

_____

_____

_____

_____

3. Why is it important to pass up small pleasures sometimes?

_____

_____

_____

_____

_____

_____

(continued)

Checkpoint (continued)

4. What are some ways to gain more skills?

_____

_____

_____

_____

_____

5. What questions should you ask yourself when you are setting short-term goals?

_____

_____

_____

_____

_____

6. How can you keep your goals realistic?

_____

_____

_____

_____

_____

7. What is an action plan?

_____

_____

_____

_____

_____

CONCLUSION

As you are working to better your life and make a career for yourself, don't forget to give yourself credit for everything you achieve.

And don't forget to make good use of your most precious resource: *your time*. Think about how you spend your time. Don't squander it!

You have many strengths, many skills, and much valuable experience already. You have a unique and important contribution to make in the workplace and in the world. When you discover yourself and what you really have to offer, the world will open up to you, and you will find what you need and what you truly want.

Appendix: Ideas of Jobs to Consider

The following jobs do not require a four-year college degree. Some people who do these jobs might have a degree or some college, but it is generally not required in these fields.

These jobs were taken from the book *America's Top Jobs® for People Without a Four-Year Degree,* also published by JIST. If you are interested in learning more about any of these jobs, that book (and others in the library) can tell you the following:

- ❏ Descriptions of what people do in these jobs

- ❏ What the working conditions are

- ❏ What skills are required to do the jobs

- ❏ Predictions of how many people will be hired into these types of jobs in the future

- ❏ Training or education you need in order to be qualified for the jobs

- ❏ How much these jobs usually pay

Actors, directors, and producers

Adjusters, investigators, and collectors

Air traffic controllers

Aircraft mechanics, including engine specialists

Aircraft pilots

Apparel workers

Automotive body repairers

Automotive mechanics

Barbers and cosmetologists

Bindery workers

Blue-collar worker supervisors

Boilermakers

Bricklayers and stonemasons

Broadcast technicians

Brokerage clerks and statement clerks

Bus drivers (municipal)

Butchers and meat, poultry, and fish cutters

Cardiovascular technologists and technicians

Carpenters

Carpet installers

Cashiers (if your conviction was not money-related)

Chefs, cooks, and other kitchen workers

Clerical supervisors and managers

Clinical laboratory technologists and technicians

Commercial and industrial electronic equipment repairers

Communications equipment mechanics

Computer and office machine repairers

Computer operators

Computer programmers

Concrete masons and terrazzo workers

Construction and building inspectors

Construction managers

Cost estimators

Counter and rental clerks

Dancers and choreographers

Dental assistants

Dental hygienists

Dental laboratory technicians

Diesel mechanics

Dispatchers

Dispensing opticians

Drafters

Drywall workers and lathers

Electric power generating plant operators and power distributors and dispatchers

Electricians

Electroneurodiagnostic technologists

Electronic equipment repairers

Electronic home entertainment equipment repairers

Elevator installers and repairers

Engineering technicians

Farm equipment mechanics

File clerks

Fishers, hunters, and trappers

Forestry and logging workers

Funeral directors

General maintenance mechanics

General office clerks

Glaziers

Handlers, equipment cleaners, helpers, and laborers

Health information technicians

Heating, air-conditioning, and refrigeration technicians

Home appliance and power tool repairers

Homemaker-home health aides

Hotel and motel desk clerks

Industrial machinery repairers

Information clerks

Inspectors and compliance officers, except construction

Inspectors, testers, and graders

Insulation workers

Insurance agents and brokers

Janitors and cleaners and cleaning supervisors

Jewelers

Library assistants and bookmobile drivers

Line installers and cable splicers

Machinists and tool programmers

Mail clerks and messengers

Manufacturers' and wholesale sales representatives

Material moving equipment operators

Material recording, scheduling, dispatching, and distributing occupations

Medical transcriptionists and stenographers

Metalworking and plastics-working machine operators

Millwrights

Mobile heavy equipment mechanics

Motorcycle, boat, and small-engine mechanics

Musical instrument repairers and tuners

Musicians

Opthalmic laboratory technicians

Order clerks

Painters and paperhangers

Payroll and time-keeping clerks

Personnel clerks

Photographers and camera operators

Photographic process operators

Plasterers

Plumbers and pipefitters

Postal clerks and mail carriers

Precision assemblers

Prepress workers

Printing press operators

Private detectives and investigators

Private household workers

Purchasers and buyers

Radiologic technicians

Rail transportation workers

Real estate agents, brokers, and appraisers

Receptionists

Record clerks

Reservation and transportation ticket agents and travel clerks

Restaurant and food service managers

Retail sales worker supervisors and managers

Retail sales workers

Roofers

Science technicians

Secretaries

Services sales representatives

Sheet-metal workers

Shoe and leather workers and repairers

Social and human service assistants

Stationary engineers

Stock clerks

Structural and reinforcing ironworkers

Surgical technologists

Surveyors and mapping scientists

Taxi drivers and chauffeurs

Telephone installers and repairers

Telephone operators

Textile machinery operators

Tilesetters

Tool and die makers

Traffic, shipping, and receiving clerks

Travel agents

Truck drivers

Typists, word processors, and data-entry keyers

Upholsterers

Vending machine servicers and repairers

Veterinary assistants and nonfarm animal caretakers

Visual artists

Water and wastewater treatment plant operators

Water transportation occupations

Welders, cutters, and welding machine operators

Woodworking occupations

JIST's *Putting the Bars Behind You* Series

by Ronald C. Mendlin and Marc Polonsky, with J. Michael Farr

The First Step to Starting Your Life Over Is to Get a Job and Keep It

One of the first things you will need to do after you are released is to find a job. But not just any job. You need to find the job that matches your skills and goals.

The five workbooks in the *Putting the Bars Behind You* series will help you discover who you are and what jobs you're good at. Then they'll help you get that job using various job-search tools. You'll even learn how to deal with the questions you dread—about your time in prison.

The final workbook in the series shows you how to keep your job, and how to keep out of prison.

Along the way, you'll get the chance to think about and use what you read. And you'll read words from real people who have been in your shoes, and see how they deal with the struggles they face.

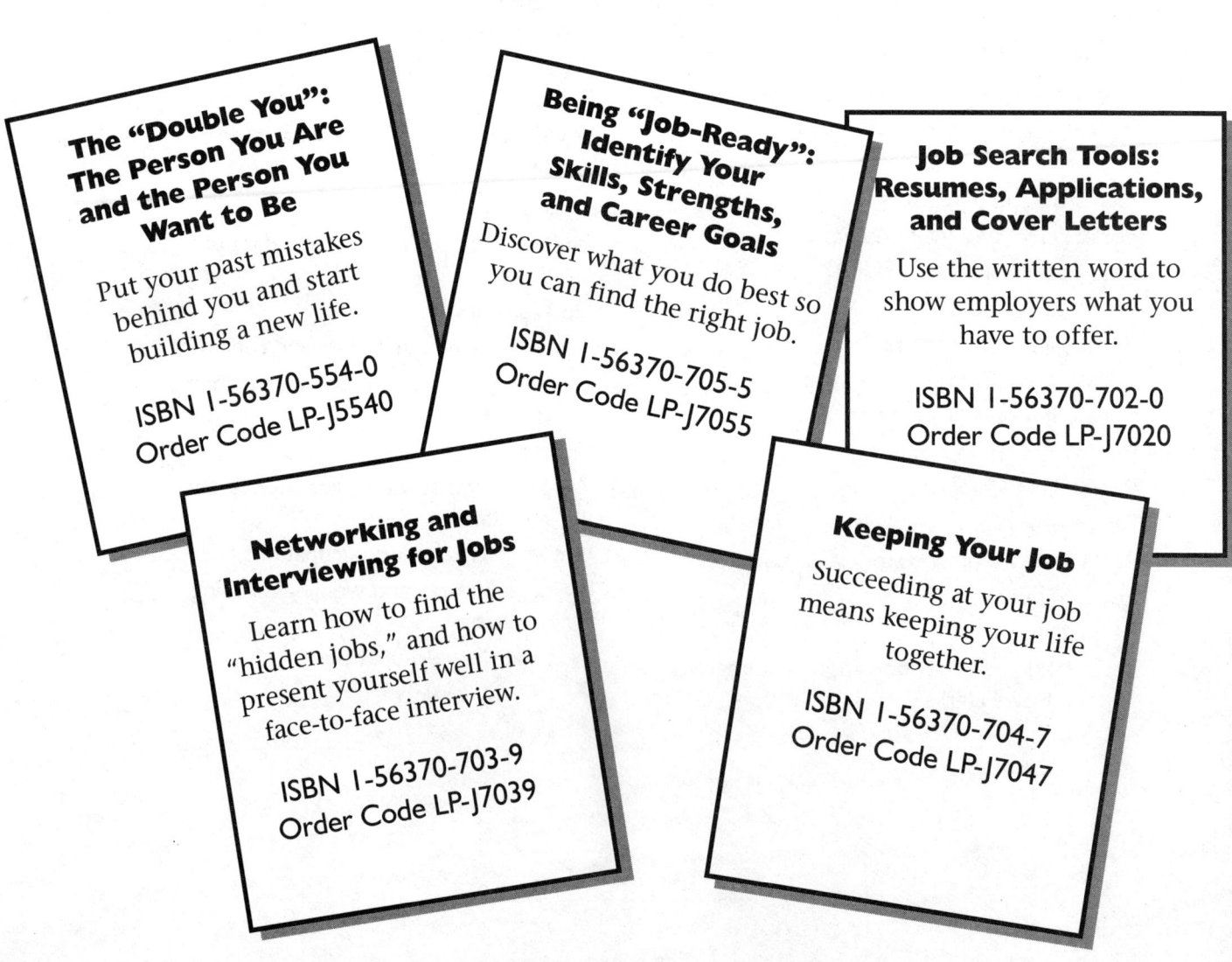

The "Double You": The Person You Are and the Person You Want to Be

Put your past mistakes behind you and start building a new life.

ISBN 1-56370-554-0
Order Code LP-J5540

Being "Job-Ready": Identify Your Skills, Strengths, and Career Goals

Discover what you do best so you can find the right job.

ISBN 1-56370-705-5
Order Code LP-J7055

Job Search Tools: Resumes, Applications, and Cover Letters

Use the written word to show employers what you have to offer.

ISBN 1-56370-702-0
Order Code LP-J7020

Networking and Interviewing for Jobs

Learn how to find the "hidden jobs," and how to present yourself well in a face-to-face interview.

ISBN 1-56370-703-9
Order Code LP-J7039

Keeping Your Job

Succeeding at your job means keeping your life together.

ISBN 1-56370-704-7
Order Code LP-J7047